# ANNUAL 2010

MERLIN: THE OFFICIAL ANNUAL 2010
A BANTAM BOOK  978 0 553 82107 9

First published in Great Britain by Bantam,
an imprint of Random House Children's Books
A Random House Group Company.

This edition published 2009

1 3 5 7 9 10 8 6 4 2

Text copyright © Bantam, 2009
© 2008 Shine Limited. Licensed by FremantleMedia Enterprises.
Merlin created by Julian Jones, Jake Michie, Julian Murphy and Johnny Capps.

Bantam Books are published by Random House Children's Books,
61–63 Uxbridge Road, London W5 5SA

www.**rbooks**.co.uk
www.**kids**at**randomhouse**.co.uk

Addresses for companies within The Random House Group Limited can be found at:
www.randomhouse.co.uk/offices.htm

THE RANDOM HOUSE GROUP Limited Reg. No. 954009

A CIP catalogue record for this book is available from the British Library

Printed in Germany

# CONTENTS

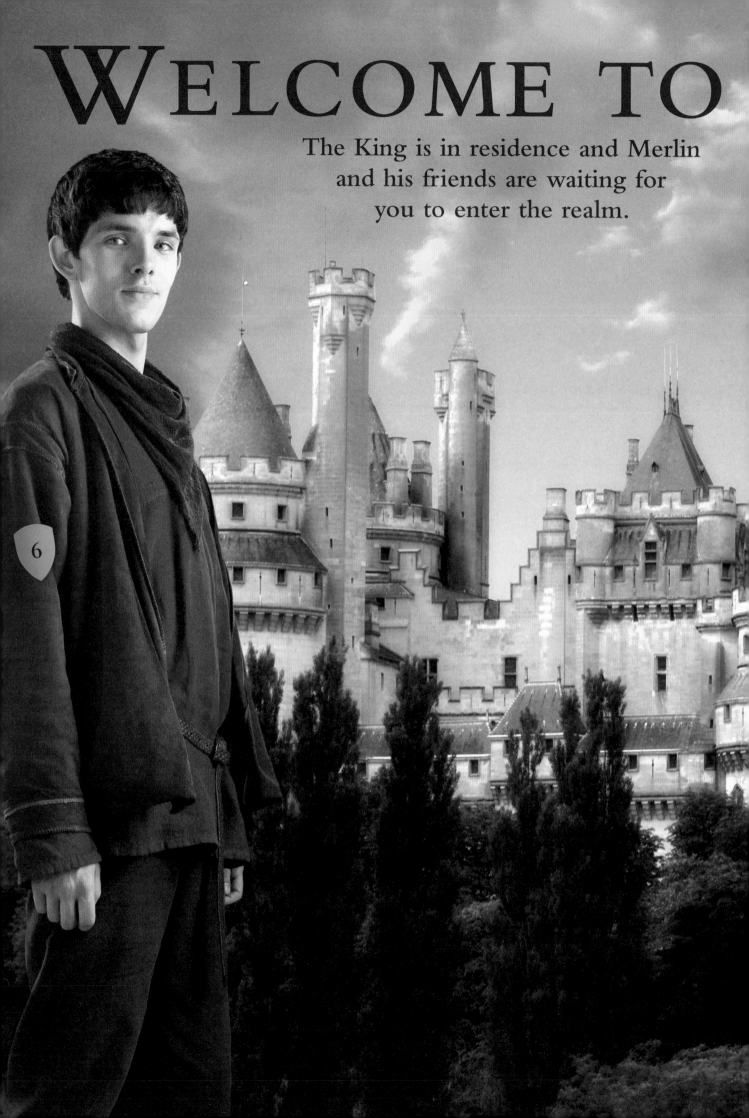

# WELCOME TO

The King is in residence and Merlin and his friends are waiting for you to enter the realm.

# CAMELOT

7

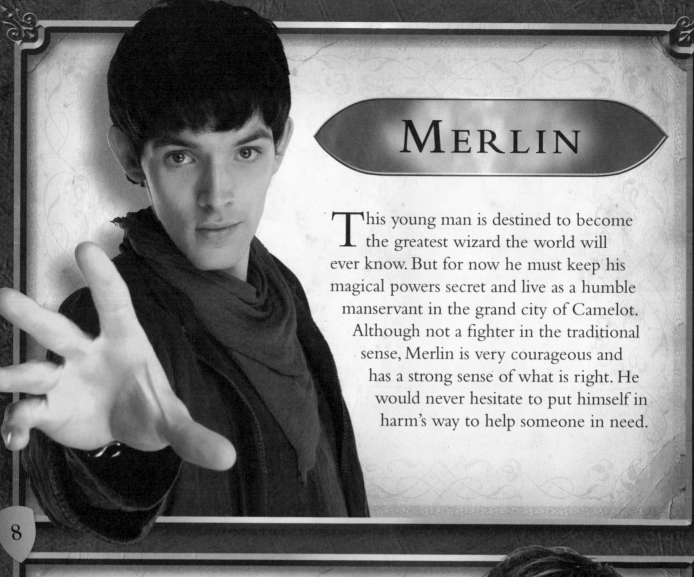

# MERLIN

This young man is destined to become the greatest wizard the world will ever know. But for now he must keep his magical powers secret and live as a humble manservant in the grand city of Camelot. Although not a fighter in the traditional sense, Merlin is very courageous and has a strong sense of what is right. He would never hesitate to put himself in harm's way to help someone in need.

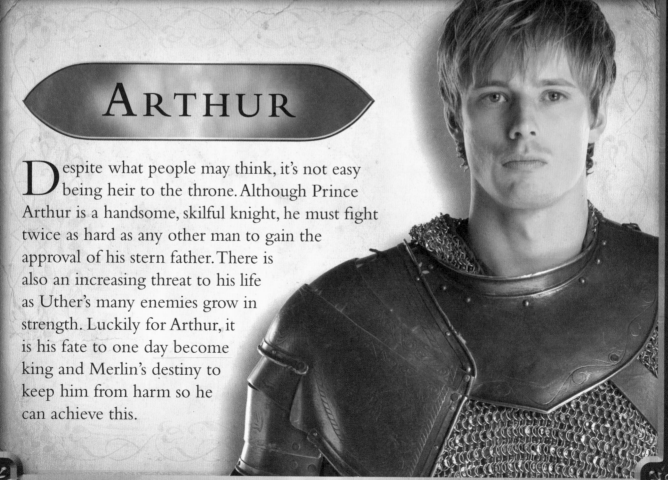

# ARTHUR

Despite what people may think, it's not easy being heir to the throne. Although Prince Arthur is a handsome, skilful knight, he must fight twice as hard as any other man to gain the approval of his stern father. There is also an increasing threat to his life as Uther's many enemies grow in strength. Luckily for Arthur, it is his fate to one day become king and Merlin's destiny to keep him from harm so he can achieve this.

# MORGANA

Renowned for her great beauty, Morgana grew up as the orphaned ward of King Uther. She offers him counsel and he occasionally listens to her advice and although Arthur would never admit it, he also listens to her reasoning. Morgana fears that sometimes her dreams predict the future but protective Gauis assures her this can't be true. Morgana's dreams certainly aren't ordinary though, so what do they mean? It seems that no one's future is more uncertain than Morgana's own . . .

# GWEN

Guinevere is the daughter of Tom, Camelot's blacksmith. She comes from a poor but loving family and works in Uther's court as Morgana's fiercely loyal maidservant. She is hardworking, has a good heart and a strong sense of right and wrong. She helps take care of Merlin and Arthur when they are both mortally ill. Her loyalty and affections for her friends run deep – but where will her destiny take her?

# MERLIN'S WORDSEARCH
Find the hidden words below.

```
S P E L L G E J L E L T S A G
N I L R E M Q K W K D R E Y I
C O U R T B J S A A R T H U R
V A L I E N U K G L U Z D D I
X H V A L I A N T A I F I R E
W R T E A U L I K N D P S U K
M O R G A N A G F C R T O D G
C D H T I N U H W E F L L E W
A R M O U R D T P L G O Y S E
M F I L R E M R U O K E I T N
E O A W I K E J A T T G N I K
L D U N G E O N U G H I A N H
O U N I C O R N J E Q E O Y K
T U E Z A M A G I C J N R N L
E H A S N A K E N M D R O W S
```

| | | | |
|---|---|---|---|
| SPELL | SIDHE | CAVE | MERLIN |
| GAIUS | DRUID | WELL | CASTLE |
| SNAKE | DESTINY | MAGIC | DRAGON |
| VALIANT | GWEN | KING | ARTHUR |
| KNIGHT | LAKE | HUNITH | FIRE |
| UTHER | LANCELOT | SWORD | |
| POTION | ARMOUR | MAZE | |
| CAMELOT | DUNGEON | COURT | |
| MORGANA | UNICORN | ALANC | |

# SPOT THE DIFFERENCE

Can you find the 10 differences between these pictures?

11

# VALIANT

It was Tournament week in Camelot and the castle was bustling with hordes of excited people. The reigning champion, Prince Arthur, was carefully inspecting his armour.

"You did all this on your own?" he asked his new servant, Merlin, in surprise.

"Yes, Sire," Merlin nodded. He'd actually put his feet up and let his magic deal with the previous day's dented shield, muddy boots, blunted sword and dirty tunic . . . but there was no way he could admit to that. He helped Arthur into his armour and handed the Prince his sword, something he'd forgotten to do the day before.

"That was much better," said Arthur. "Not that it could have got any worse."

Merlin smiled through gritted teeth, wished his master luck and followed him to the tournament ground.

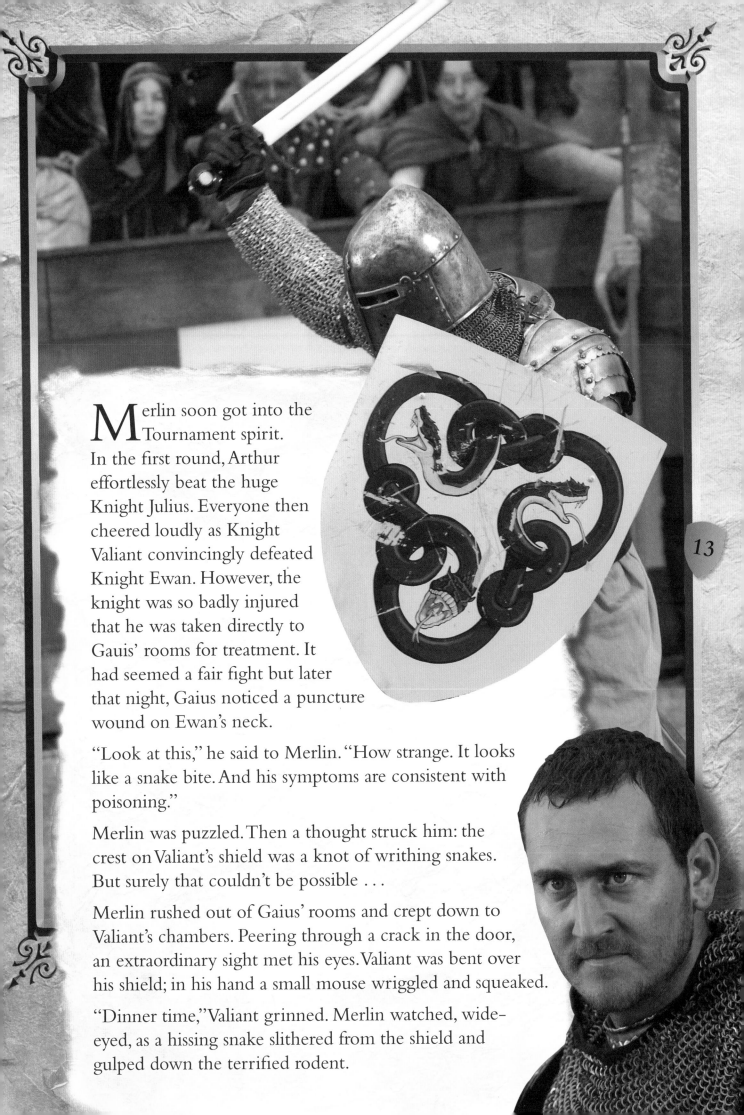

Merlin soon got into the Tournament spirit. In the first round, Arthur effortlessly beat the huge Knight Julius. Everyone then cheered loudly as Knight Valiant convincingly defeated Knight Ewan. However, the knight was so badly injured that he was taken directly to Gauis' rooms for treatment. It had seemed a fair fight but later that night, Gaius noticed a puncture wound on Ewan's neck.

"Look at this," he said to Merlin. "How strange. It looks like a snake bite. And his symptoms are consistent with poisoning."

Merlin was puzzled. Then a thought struck him: the crest on Valiant's shield was a knot of writhing snakes. But surely that couldn't be possible . . .

Merlin rushed out of Gaius' rooms and crept down to Valiant's chambers. Peering through a crack in the door, an extraordinary sight met his eyes. Valiant was bent over his shield; in his hand a small mouse wriggled and squeaked.

"Dinner time," Valiant grinned. Merlin watched, wide-eyed, as a hissing snake slithered from the shield and gulped down the terrified rodent.

13

Now Merlin knew the dark secret behind Valiant's victory. He ran back to Gaius to tell him.

"Are you sure?" asked the court physician. Merlin was hurt.

"Don't you believe me?" he asked.

"Yes," Gaius assured him. "But you can't accuse a knight without proof. The King will never accept the word of a servant. There's nothing you can do."

"But Arthur fights Valiant tomorrow!" cried Merlin, "We have to do something!"

Gaius thought long and hard. Uther would only believe such an accusation if it came from Ewan himself. He needed an antidote, and he needed it quickly if Ewan were to stand witness against the rogue knight. Merlin knew what he must do. Returning to Valiant's empty chambers he bent close over the shield. As a snake slithered towards Merlin's face, he grabbed a sword from the table and cleanly sliced through its neck. The severed head squirmed on the floor, then was still. He picked it up and made his escape.

Valiant stood unseen in the shadowy passageway and watched as Merlin rushed past.

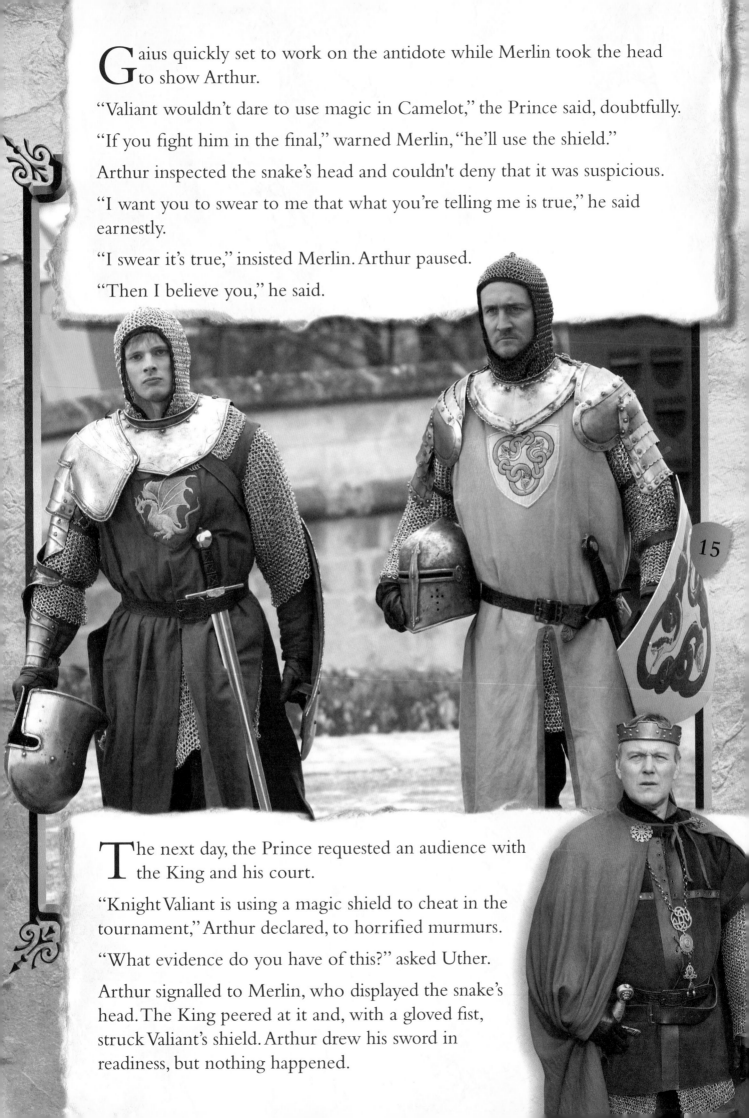

Gaius quickly set to work on the antidote while Merlin took the head to show Arthur.

"Valiant wouldn't dare to use magic in Camelot," the Prince said, doubtfully.

"If you fight him in the final," warned Merlin, "he'll use the shield."

Arthur inspected the snake's head and couldn't deny that it was suspicious.

"I want you to swear to me that what you're telling me is true," he said earnestly.

"I swear it's true," insisted Merlin. Arthur paused.

"Then I believe you," he said.

The next day, the Prince requested an audience with the King and his court.

"Knight Valiant is using a magic shield to cheat in the tournament," Arthur declared, to horrified murmurs.

"What evidence do you have of this?" asked Uther.

Arthur signalled to Merlin, who displayed the snake's head. The King peered at it and, with a gloved fist, struck Valiant's shield. Arthur drew his sword in readiness, but nothing happened.

"As you see, my Lord, it's just an ordinary shield," smirked Valiant.

Arthur kept his calm; he just needed his witness.

"Where's Ewan?" he whispered to Merlin.

Merlin hurried over to Gaius, but he had grim news: Ewan had suffered another snake bite and had died in the night.

"So you have no proof of these allegations?" scowled Uther, impatiently.

"No," replied Arthur. "But my servant fought these snakes . . . "

"You're making wild accusations against a knight on the word of your servant?" The King was incredulous.

"I'm not lying!" Merlin blurted out.

"How dare you interrupt," roared the King. "Seize him!"

The guards began to lead Merlin away, but Valiant insisted that he be freed.

"My Lord, if your son made these accusations because he's afraid to fight me," he sneered, "then I'll graciously accept his withdrawal."

Arthur was humiliated; there was no way he was going to concede defeat in the Tournament. He had no choice but to withdraw his allegation and apologize.

Arthur dismissed his servant for good and stormed off to his chambers in a rage. Merlin sat brooding on the castle steps. Frustrated as he was, there was no way he could let Arthur walk to his death in the morning. But what could he do? His gaze came to rest on the statue of a dog.

"That's it!" he exclaimed. With some effort he managed to get the statue back to his room. He leafed through the pages of the Book of Magic until he found the spell he was looking for ...

17

Merlin spent the whole night chanting the incantation, but the statue remained lifeless.

As day dawned, he began to give up. Exhausted, he muttered the spell one last time. Suddenly, from the foot of his bed, he heard a low growl and felt a leathery tongue lick his foot.

"I did it!" he gasped. By the door sat a huge, slavering hound. He raced to the tournament; the final was already underway.

The sound of sword striking shield greeted Merlin at the tournament ground. The two knights were battling fiercely. Arthur delivered a powerful blow that sent Valiant's helmet rolling across the ground. Chivalrously, Arthur removed his own helmet but at that moment Valiant lunged forward, striking him so forcefully with his shield that Arthur dropped his sword. Seizing the moment, Valiant bore down on his opponent. Using all his might, he pinned Arthur beneath his shield against the side of the arena. Gathering his strength, Arthur sent his opponent staggering backwards. Seeing his chance, Merlin uttered the enchanted words. The dark green snakes slithered forth for all to see. Cries of shock came from the watching crowd.

"He *is* using magic," said Uther, aghast.

Seeing that he had nothing to lose, Valiant ran forward with his shield raised and snakes writhing to kill the defenceless Arthur.

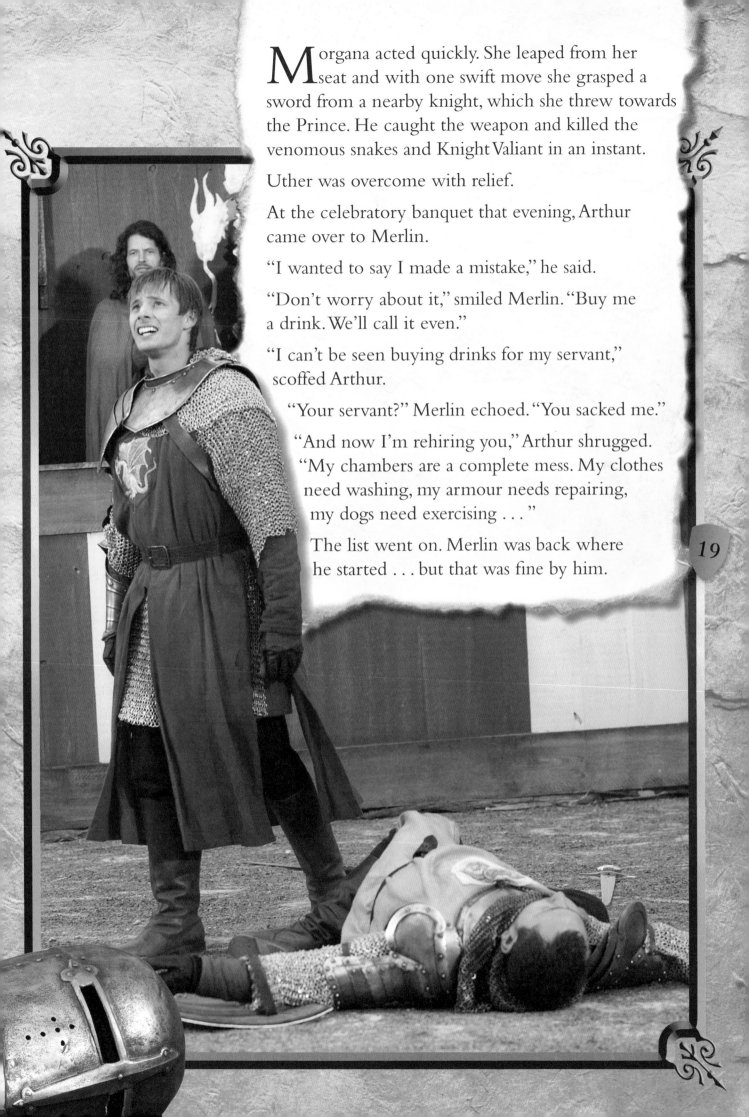

Morgana acted quickly. She leaped from her seat and with one swift move she grasped a sword from a nearby knight, which she threw towards the Prince. He caught the weapon and killed the venomous snakes and Knight Valiant in an instant.

Uther was overcome with relief.

At the celebratory banquet that evening, Arthur came over to Merlin.

"I wanted to say I made a mistake," he said.

"Don't worry about it," smiled Merlin. "Buy me a drink. We'll call it even."

"I can't be seen buying drinks for my servant," scoffed Arthur.

"Your servant?" Merlin echoed. "You sacked me."

"And now I'm rehiring you," Arthur shrugged. "My chambers are a complete mess. My clothes need washing, my armour needs repairing, my dogs need exercising . . ."

The list went on. Merlin was back where he started . . . but that was fine by him.

19

# A Knight's Colours

As Arthur won each round of the tournament, his colours moved up the scoreboard until he was crowned champion – no thanks to cheating Valiant!

Use your pens or pencils to design your own shield here.

What would your knight's colours be?

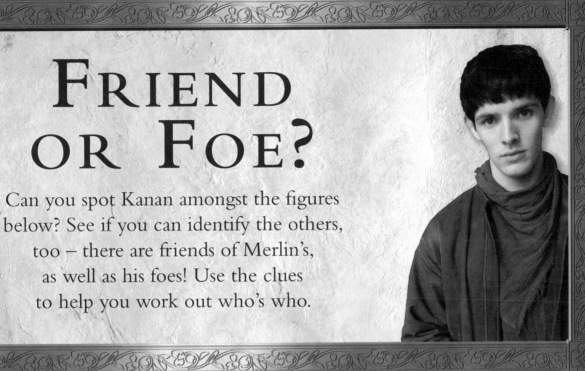

# FRIEND OR FOE?

Can you spot Kanan amongst the figures below? See if you can identify the others, too – there are friends of Merlin's, as well as his foes! Use the clues to help you work out who's who.

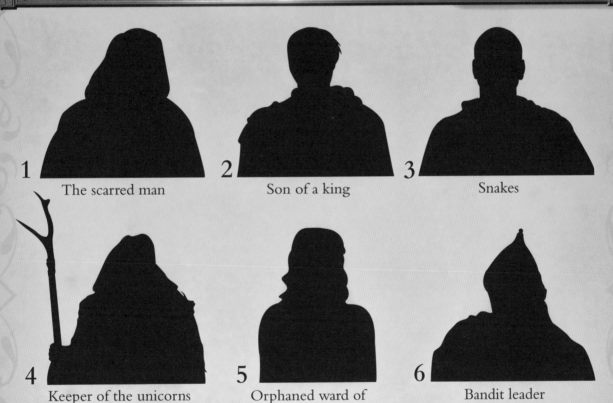

**1**   The scarred man

**2**   Son of a king

**3**   Snakes

**4**   Keeper of the unicorns

**5**   Orphaned ward of King Uther

**6**   Bandit leader

**7**   Merlin's guardian

**8**   A very powerful sorceress

**9**   Maidservant to Morgana

# WHO ARE YOU MOST LIKE?

Imagine you live in Merlin's time. Are you courageous but unassuming like him, or confidently brave like Arthur? Maybe you're a little bit rebellious, like Morgana, or gentle and hardworking like Gwen? Try these questions and make a note of whether you answer mainly a's, b's, c's or d's to see which of the four you are most like!

## 1. How are your fighting skills?

a) Brilliant.
b) Good.
c) To be used in emergencies only.
d) Not bad.

## 2. You see a unicorn whilst in the forest. What do you do?

a) Hunt it down.
b) Keep it as a much-loved pet.
c) Stroke it and let it go.
d) Watch it from a distance.

## 3. How would you treat a servant if you had one?

a) Like a servant!
b) Like a welcome helping hand.
c) I wouldn't want a servant.
d) Like a friend.

## 4. Are you interested in magic?

a) No, not at all.
b) I'm a little fascinated by it.
c) Secretly, yes.
d) I'm a little afraid of it.

## 5. What do you think of rules and regulations?

a) They should mostly be followed.
b) They should mostly be ignored.
c) They should sometimes be bent… just a little.
d) They should always be followed.

## 6. What keeps you awake at night?

a) Nothing.
b) Strange dreams.
c) Reading for too long.
d) Worrying about my family.

## 7. What's your greatest weapon?

a) My sword.
b) My way with words.
c) My magic.
d) My smile.

## 8. Do you think that you're good-looking?

a) Yes, very.
b) Reasonably.
c) No.
d) I'm not sure.

## 9. Do you keep your bedroom tidy?

a) Someone else does it for me.
b) Yes, reasonably.
c) Not at all.
d) Yes – and everyone else's too.

## 10. What is your greatest fear?

a) I fear nothing.
b) Harm coming to those I love.
c) Not fulfilling my destiny.
d) Losing my family.

## 11. How often do you read?

a) Only when necessary.
b) Often.
c) Every day.
d) I'm too busy to read.

## 12. How do you speak to your parents?

a) With respect.
b) With humour.
c) With affection.
d) With love.

55

### Mostly a's

A is for all the action, which is what you like to be in the middle of – just like Arthur! Although you have respect for authority, you are confident and fearless, but can be a little insensitive at times too.

### Mostly b's

B is for bold as brass. Like strong-willed Morgana, you don't like being told what to do and will usually get your own way in the end. You also have a softer side, though, and make a loyal companion.

### Mostly c's

C is for calmness, which is what you bring to any volatile situation. You share Merlin's gentleness, curiosity and modesty, but also his hidden strength and courage to do what you think is right.

### Mostly d's

D is for decent and dedicated. You are a giving person, with the same work ethic as Gwen, and no task is too much if it means helping others. Don't overdo it, though – you should also find time for yourself now and again.

# NIMUEH

When magic alone could give Queen Ygraine a son, Nimueh was welcome in Camelot. That changed when the Queen died after Arthur's birth – the witch was banished and all of her kind were executed. Now her sole aim is to destroy King Uther and his kingdom.

# THE BLACK KNIGHT

Nimueh uses her magic to raise the spirit of Tristan de Bois, Ygraine's brother. The indestructible Black Knight is due to fight Arthur when Merlin reads in an ancient text that only a sword forged in a dragon's breath can destroy the wraith.

# THE AFANC

A powerful beast with razor-sharp teeth, the Afanc is originally moulded from clay by Nimueh and sent into Camelot's water supply inside a magical egg. Once brought to life and released, the monster grows to spread its lethal poison and wreak havoc on the city.

# THE VISITOR

Where did Valiant come from? To find out, do the sums on these banners to see which number each letter stands for. Then write your letters in the correct spaces below. The answer is at the back of your annual.

$18 - 11$ = H7

$3 + 6$ = E9

$19 - 14$ = W5

$9 + 5$ = T14

$6 + 2$ = S8

$17 - 6$ = R11

$15 - 12$ = N3

$8 + 8$ = I16

$16 - 4$ = L12

21

T h e    w e s t e r n    I s l e s
14 7 9    5 9 8 14 9 11 3    16 8 12 9 8

# A Knight's Shield

A knight's shield can get easily damaged so the blacksmith makes him plenty of replacements. Look carefully at the shields below, can you spot the one that the blacksmith got wrong?

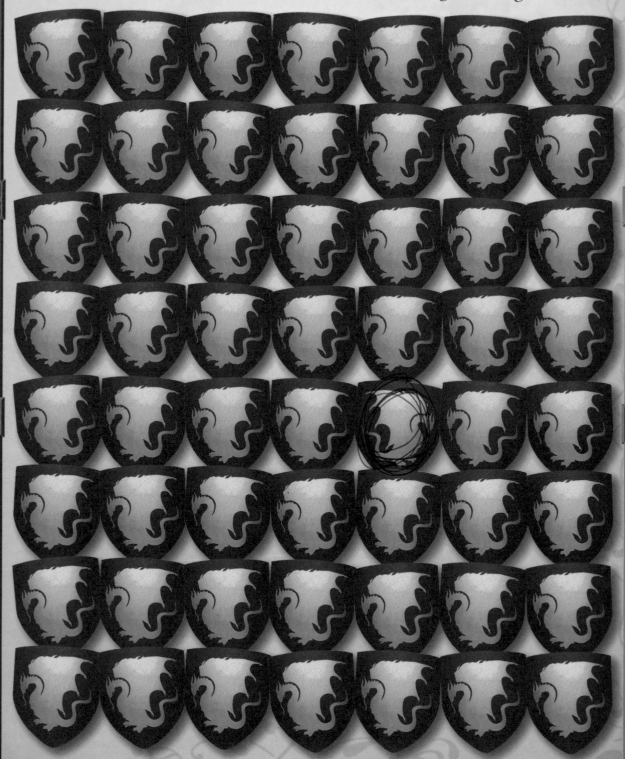

# WINNING COLOURS

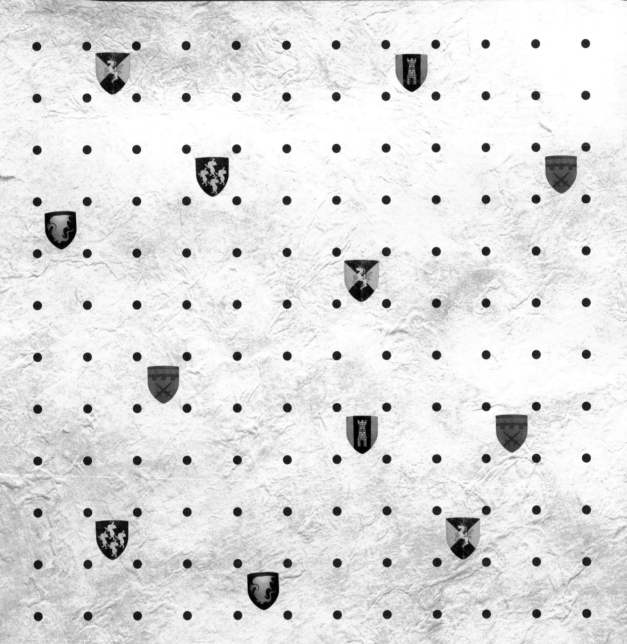

Play this game with a friend to see who can get the most squares, scoring extra points for shields. All you need to do is take turns to join two dots with a vertical or horizontal line. If your line completes a square, write your initials inside it. Score 5 points for a regular square and 10 points for a shield square. The person with the most points once all the squares are completed is the winner!

# WORD SNAKE

Look at the letters in the snake below and see if you can find some of the character's names. Which name do the leftover letters spell?

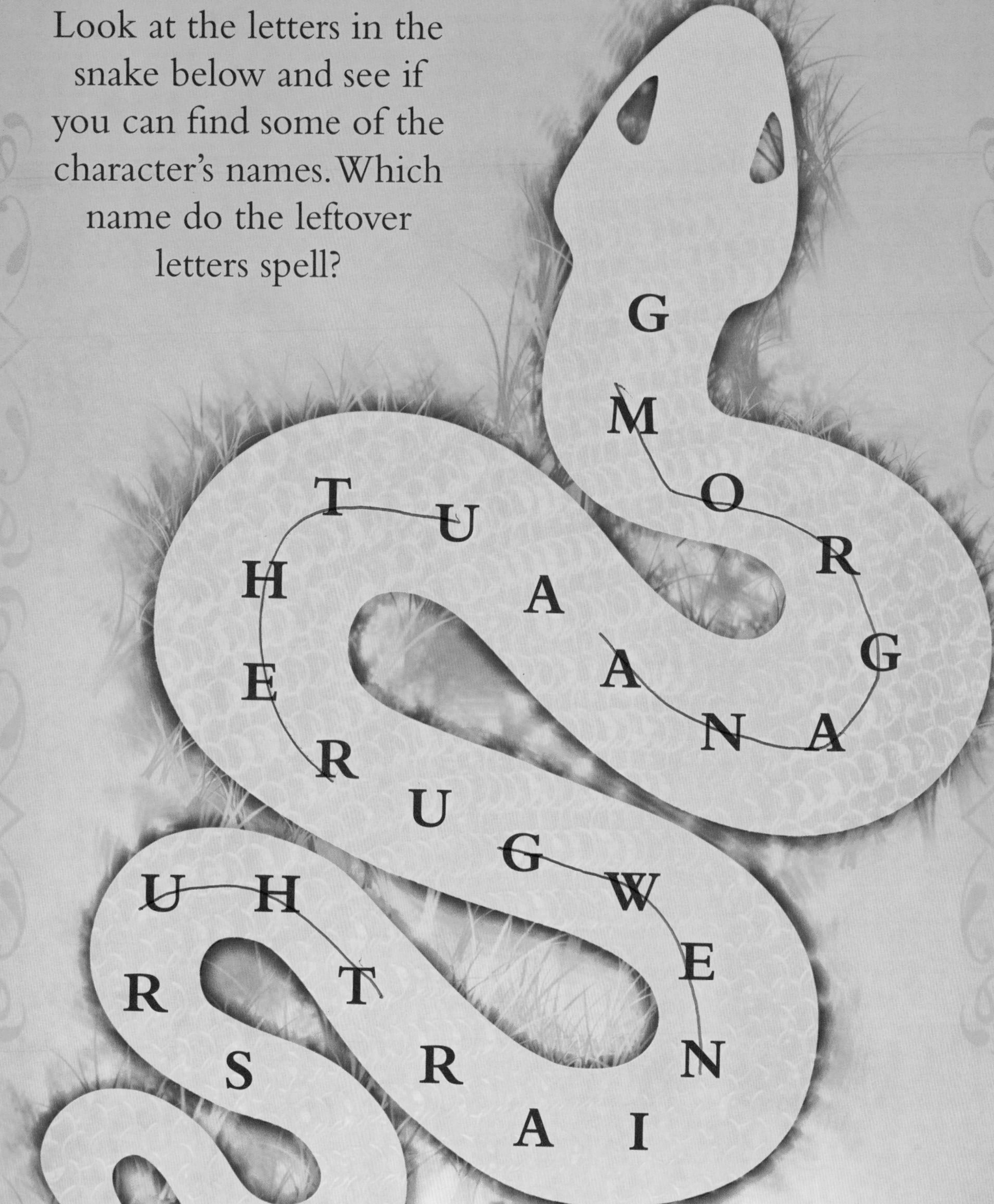

24

G
M
O
R
G
T
U
H
A
A
E
N
A
R
U
G
U
H
W
R
T
E
S
R
N
A
I

# LANCELOT LETTERS

How many words can you make from the letters in Lancelot's name? You can use each letter no more than once for each word. The first one is done for you – see if you can make it to twenty!

# LANCELOT

1. coat
2. cat
3. LOL
4. ~~let~~ lot
5. A
6. an
7. can
8. lot
9. .............
10. .............

11. .............
12. .............
13. .............
14. .............
15. .............
16. .............
17. .............
18. .............
19. .............
20. .............

# GAIUS

As court physician, kind-hearted Gaius has the job of looking after the people of Camelot. When an old friend sends her son to stay with him, Gaius takes Merlin under his wing. As a former follower of the old religion Gaius is impressed as well as being slightly concerned by Merlin's natural flair for magic. He takes it upon himself to guide and protect Merlin from Uther's attempt to rid the kingdom of magic and all who practise it.

# UTHER

Uther rules Camelot with an iron fist. He despises magic and all who use it, sentencing anyone he finds guilty of practising it to death. Although magic brought him his son Arthur, he was left grief-stricken when his beloved wife died after giving birth. His intolerance of all enchantment means that good magic has been driven out with the bad, leaving Camelot vulnerable to evil.

# LANCELOT

Lancelot has dreamt of becoming a knight ever since he was a boy and his parents were killed in an attack on his village. He arrives in Camelot to offer his services, nobly and fearlessly entering into battle against a Griffin, to protect Merlin. However, to become a knight Lancelot must also be from a noble background and his humble roots mean that his fighting skills alone are not enough to help him achieve his dream.

# THE GREAT DRAGON

During Uther's purge of magic, all the dragons in the land were slaughtered, except one. Chained in a cavern deep beneath Camelot lives the Great Dragon. He is centuries old and has the ability to prophesy the future. He tries to guide Merlin towards his destiny and offers advice in his hour of need but his heart's desire is to be free, at any cost.

# THE LABYRINTH OF GEDREF

Camelot was in crisis: all its crops had died suddenly and the water pumps were running with nothing but sand. Gaius had done his best to find a scientific explanation, but there was none.

"I can only conclude that these events are the result of sorcery," he told Uther.

"You are right," agreed the King. "The kingdom is under attack."

Uther immediately issued a decree that looters would be executed and placed his city under curfew.

"Without food or water, we will not survive for long," he said to Arthur. "You must find whoever is responsible and put an end to this."

"Yes, Father," nodded Arthur.

Merlin, however, knew who was responsible: Arthur had killed a unicorn whilst out hunting and according to legend, bad fortune would come to anyone who slayed one. The kill had upset Merlin, since he'd felt privileged to see such a rare and beautiful creature.

As the curfew began that evening, Arthur and Merlin caught a glimpse of a hooded figure entering the castle vaults. They followed and tried to cut the intruder off in the passageways, but he seemed to have vanished. The two were startled when he suddenly reappeared behind them.

"Who are you?" asked Arthur.

"I am Anhora," replied the cloaked man, "keeper of the unicorns. You alone are responsible for the misfortune that has befallen Camelot."

"Me?" echoed Arthur, incredulously. "You think I would bring famine and drought upon my own people?"

"When you killed the unicorn, you unleashed a curse," Anhora explained. "For this, Camelot will suffer greatly."

"Undo the curse, or face execution," Arthur threatened.

"Only you can do that," said the sorcerer, remaining calm. "You will be tested. If you fail, Camelot will be damned for all eternity."

Arthur lunged forward to grab Anhora, but he was gone.

Arthur was not convinced; he held Anhora responsible for the curse and vowed to track him down. All the city had left was its stock of grain and, believing that was where the sorcerer would strike next, Arthur lay in wait by the store.

"Someone's coming," he whispered to Merlin. He crept up on the cloaked man leaning over the grain sacks and levelled a sword at his back.

"Show yourself, before I run you through," the Prince ordered.

When the figure turned, they were surprised to see it was a terrified villager.

"Please, my Lord," he begged. "I do not steal for myself. I have three children…they are hungry."

Arthur softened. Although his father had ordered that looters be executed, he let the poor man go with some grain for his family.

"You have shown yourself to be merciful and kind," the man added, as he left. "This will bring its own reward."

The next day, water returned to the kingdom.

"I never thought water could taste so good," sighed Arthur, between gulps from his tankard.

"What if last night was your first test?" asked Merlin, thinking about what the villager had said about a reward. "You passed it, so the curse has begun to lift."

Arthur was doubtful, but Merlin knew he was right and carried on.

"If you're tested again, you have a chance to end your people's suffering. Perhaps we should find Anhora."

"I cannot negotiate with sorcerers," Arthur interrupted. "My father will not hear of it."

Merlin returned to the forest alone and called out to Anhora to show himself.

"You wanted to speak with me?" asked Anhora, appearing behind him.

"I have come to seek your help," said Merlin. "The people are starving. Give Arthur another chance – he will prove himself worthy and lift the curse."

Anhora sensed the strength of Merlin's loyalty.

"You have faith in Arthur?" he asked.

"I trust him with my life," nodded Merlin. The old sorcerer paused for a few moments.

"Arthur must go to the Labyrinth of Gedref," he said at last. "There, he will face a final test. If he fails, the curse will destroy Camelot." With that, he vanished.

Arthur was desperate to save his people and had no choice but to take the test. Not knowing what lay in store, he set off the next morning and ordered Merlin to stay behind. He rode for miles through woodland until he could make out the vast Labyrinth of Gedref in the misty valley below. Once he had crossed the valley, he slipped down from his horse and tethered it beside the maze entrance. Uncertainly, he stepped inside and gingerly made his way back and forth through the eerie labyrinth.

After many twists, turns and dead ends, Arthur finally found a large, light opening in the maze. He could hear the lapping of waves and walked through to see Anhora standing on a rocky shore. Beside him was a wooden table laid with two silver goblets. Sitting sheepishly at one end was Merlin – he had followed his master into the maze, but was caught by Anhora.

"I thought I told you to stay in Camelot," scolded Arthur, taking a seat at the table to face his servant.

"I must have misheard you," Merlin lied.

"Let's get on with it," said Arthur, glaring at Anhora.

"There are two goblets before you," the sorcerer explained. "One contains a deadly poison, the other a harmless liquid. All the liquid in both goblets must be drunk, but each of you may only drink from a single goblet."

Arthur was highly agitated, but Merlin studied the goblets thoughtfully.

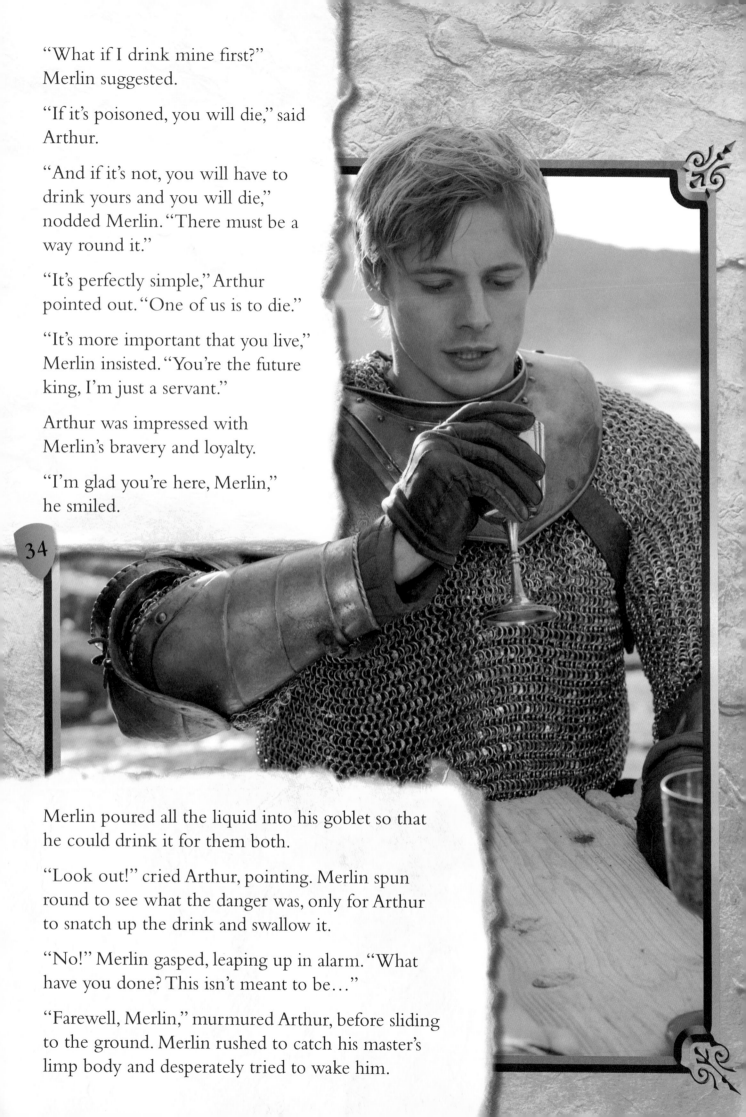

"What if I drink mine first?" Merlin suggested.

"If it's poisoned, you will die," said Arthur.

"And if it's not, you will have to drink yours and you will die," nodded Merlin. "There must be a way round it."

"It's perfectly simple," Arthur pointed out. "One of us is to die."

"It's more important that you live," Merlin insisted. "You're the future king, I'm just a servant."

Arthur was impressed with Merlin's bravery and loyalty.

"I'm glad you're here, Merlin," he smiled.

34

Merlin poured all the liquid into his goblet so that he could drink it for them both.

"Look out!" cried Arthur, pointing. Merlin spun round to see what the danger was, only for Arthur to snatch up the drink and swallow it.

"No!" Merlin gasped, leaping up in alarm. "What have you done? This isn't meant to be…"

"Farewell, Merlin," murmured Arthur, before sliding to the ground. Merlin rushed to catch his master's limp body and desperately tried to wake him.

"He cannot die," Merlin told Anhora, distraught. "I will take his place!"

"This was the test," said the sorcerer, gently. "He has merely consumed a sleeping draught and will come round shortly. A unicorn is pure of heart. If you kill one, you must make amends by proving that you also are pure of heart. Arthur was willing to sacrifice his life to save yours. The curse will be lifted."

Once Arthur groaned and began to move, Anhora was gone.

By the time the pair got back to Camelot, the crops were healthy once again – the curse had indeed been lifted.

"Is this your doing?" Uther asked eagerly, hurrying up to his son. "Is the sorcerer dead?"

"He will not be troubling us again," Arthur replied with confidence. Merlin smiled; he would keep his promise not to tell anyone that the Prince was willing to give his life for that of a servant…

# NUMBER STONES

Look at the numbers on these stones. See if you can fill in the empty bricks – the number in each one is the sum of the two stones directly underneath it. Check your answers with those on page 61!

# CROSSWORD

See if you can remember the story well enough to answer these clues and complete the crossword. The solution is at the back of your annual.

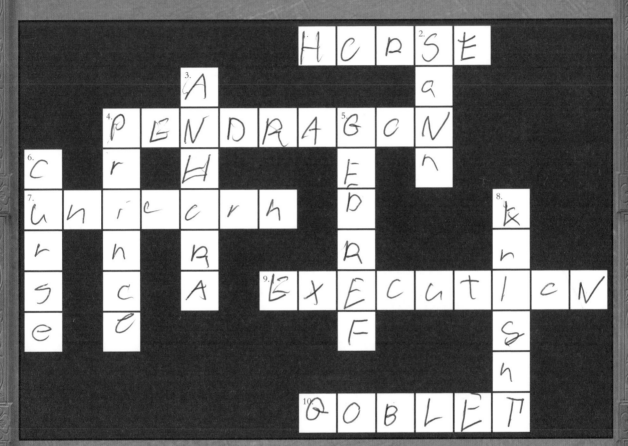

## Across

**1.** Arthur's mode of transport *(5)*

**4.** Arthur's surname *(9)*

**7.** The creature that Arthur killed *(7)*

**9.** The punishment for looters *(9)*

**10.** The vessel that Arthur drank from *(6)*

## Down

**2.** What came from the pumps instead of water *(4)*

**3.** Keeper of the unicorns *(6)*

**4.** Arthur's royal title *(6)*

**5.** The name of the labyrinth where Arthur was tested *(6)*

**6.** Arthur was willing to give his life to undo this *(5)*

**8.** A nobleman who fights for the King *(6)*

# MERLIN MAGIC

Do you know your Questing Beast from your Cockatrice? Are you smart enough to be a wizard yourself? Do this quiz to see how much you really know about Merlin's adventures! Check your answers with those at the bottom of the page and give yourself a point for each correct one so you can see what your sorcerer score is.

## 1

What job does Gaius hold in Camelot?

a) Court adviser........ ☐
b) Court jester.......... ☐
c) Court physician..... ☑

38

## 2

The bite of which creature is said to be always fatal?

a) The unicorn.......... ☐
b) The Questing Beast. ☐
c) The scarab beetle..... ☑

## 3

Which group of magic people does Mordred belong to?

a) Druids........ ☑
b) Sidhe.......... ☐
c) Changelings.. ☐

## 4

When Camelot was cursed with a food shortage, what did Merlin cook for Arthur?

a) Gruel............. ☐
b) Rat stew......... ☑
c) Cabbage soup... ☐

## 5

What did Nimueh disguise herself as to get into Camelot?

a) A beggar............. ☑
b) A servant .......... ☐
c) An old woman..... ☐

## 6

Which knight saved Merlin from a Griffin?

a) Galahad.... ☐
b) Arthur...... ☐
c) Lancelot.... ☑

## 7

What did Gaius need to make a snake bite antidote?

a) Snake venom.... ☐ ✗
b) Snake blood..... ☑
c) Snake skin....... ☐

## 10

How many goblets awaited Arthur in the Labyrinth of Gedref?

a) One...... ☐ ✓
b) Two...... ☑
c) Three..... ☐

## 8

Which insect did Edwin use in his spell to make Morgana sick?

a) A honeybee......... ☐
b) A ladybird.......... ☐
c) An Elanthia beetle ☑ ✓

## 11

What was Kanan's weapon of choice?

a) A battleaxe...... ☑ ✓
b) A longbow....... ☐
c) A broadsword ... ☐

## 12

Tauren asked for help from Gwen's father to do what?

a) Turn water into wine........ ☐
b) Turn sand into diamonds... ☐
c) Turn lead into gold......... ☑ ✓

39

## 9

How was the Black Knight related to Arthur? ✓

a) He was Arthur's brother........ ☐
b) He was Arthur's uncle.......... ☑
c) He was Arthur's grandfather... ☐

# What's your sorcerer score?

**10 or more:** You don't miss much and would make a star sorcerer like Merlin!

**(5-9:)** Not bad, but you'll have to pay more attention if you want to make it in magic.

**4 or less:** You're not quite ready to be a wizard yet. Better luck next time!

9
12

# EDWIN

When a mysterious physician arrives in Camelot with a cure for all ills, it seems that Gaius is no longer needed. In reality, Edwin is there to settle a score: his sorcerer parents were burnt to death during the Great Purge and he was scarred for life trying to save them.

# TAUREN

The Order of Four is a band of renegade sorcerers sworn to bring down the King. As its leader, Tauren is delighted to get an offer of help from an unexpected source. Morgana is seeking a way to get her own back on Uther after he had Gwen's father killed and sees this as the perfect opportunity.

# MARY COLLINS

The son of this old sorceress was executed in King Uther's purge of magic… and she is now out for revenge. Her enchanted pendant gives her the ability to shape-shift and use magic to help her take from Uther what he took from her: a son for a son.

# MEDICINE MUDDLE

When Edwin secretly used an enchanted scarab to make Morgana gravely ill, Gaius tried to cure her with potions made from herbs. Put the letters in the right order to find out which herb is in each of his jars. The answers are on page 61.

1 tin m

_ _ _ _

2 more yars

_ _ _ _ _ _ _

3 ge as

_ _ _ _ _

4 vealr end

_ _ _ _ _ _ _

5 hem yt

_ _ _ _ _

41

# EALDOR

As the sun rose over the village of Ealdor, Merlin helped Arthur into his armour.

"Have you still not learnt how to dress yourself?" Morgana teased.

"You don't have a dog and fetch the stick yourself," said Arthur. "No offence, Merlin."

"None taken," Merlin smiled. He could hardly believe that the Prince was here, in the young wizard's tiny family home. Morgana and Gwen had come with him too. The band of friends were determined to help defeat the vicious bandits who had been raiding the village and would soon be back for what was left of the harvest.

"Prince Arthur, you didn't finish your breakfast," said Merlin's mother, holding out a bowl of unappetising gruel.

"Didn't I?" Arthur said politely. He took the bowl and, as soon as Hunith's back was turned, passed it to Gwen.

"Let's get going, Merlin," he urged. "We're going to need wood, lots of it."

Morgana and Gwen worked with the women of the village, sharpening weapon blades, while Arthur used thick branches to teach the men how to fight with swords. Merlin was chopping wood, when his old friend Will came and sat on a tree trunk next to him.

"You'd be able to defeat Kanan on your own, wouldn't you?" he asked knowingly.

"Not sure," Merlin replied; Kanan was a terrifying and ruthless warrior. "Maybe."

"What's stopping you?" asked Will. "So what if Arthur finds out?"

Merlin knew William hated the nobility; his father had died fighting for a king.

"One day, Arthur will be a great king," Merlin explained, "but he needs my help. If people found out about my powers, I'd have to leave Camelot for good."

Will studied him, appalled.

"So you'd rather keep your magic secret for Arthur's sake than use it to protect your friends and family?" he asked.

Merlin looked away, troubled by this dilemma.

The next day, Arthur was announcing his battle strategy to the villagers when he was interrupted by a scream. He was horrified to see a horse approaching with a man's body slumped across its back: it was Matthew, who had been on sentry duty.

"Get him down from there," Arthur ordered gently. Merlin and the villagers lay Matthew on the ground, revealing a crossbow bolt in his back with a note attached to it.

"Make the most of this day, it will be your last," Arthur read aloud. Matthew's wife fought her way through the crowd and knelt weeping over his body.

"You did this," spat Will. "You've killed him!"

"It wasn't his fault," Merlin tried to defend his master.

"If he wasn't strutting around treating this like his own personal army, it would never have happened!" Will shouted. "These men aren't soldiers, they're farmers!"

"This battle can be won," insisted Arthur. "It will be won!"

Will, however, was sure the village faced slaughter and stormed home to pack.

That night, Arthur told the villagers that the women and children should leave the village early the next morning to take refuge in the woods.

"We're not going anywhere," declared Gwen. "The women have as much right to fight as the men."

Seeing several women stand next to Gwen in agreement, Arthur realised their minds were made up.

"This is your home," he nodded. "If you want to defend it, that's your choice. He turned to the rest of the crowd. "You fight for your friends and family. You fight for the right to grow crops in peace. If you fall, you fall fighting for the noblest of causes – fighting for your lives! For Ealdor!"

"For Ealdor!" the villagers cried in unison, confidently raising their swords. Will watched glumly from a distance, before disappearing into the darkness, a bag slung over his shoulder.

The next morning, Merlin went to help Arthur with his armour as usual.

"No, not today," said Arthur, stopping him. "Put on your own."

When they were both ready for battle, Merlin took a deep breath.

"Whatever happens out there today, please don't think any differently of me," he said.

"It's all right to be scared, Merlin," Arthur assured him.

"That's not what I meant," said Merlin; he was sure that only his magic could get them through this. Before he could reveal his secret, there was a shout from Morgana: Kanan and his men were approaching on horseback.

46

Arthur and the villagers lay in wait behind a wall. It wasn't long before they heard battle cries from the advancing bandits. Arthur held everyone back, even as the scar-faced Kanan and his men rode into the seemingly deserted village.

"Come out, come out, wherever you are," growled Kanan.

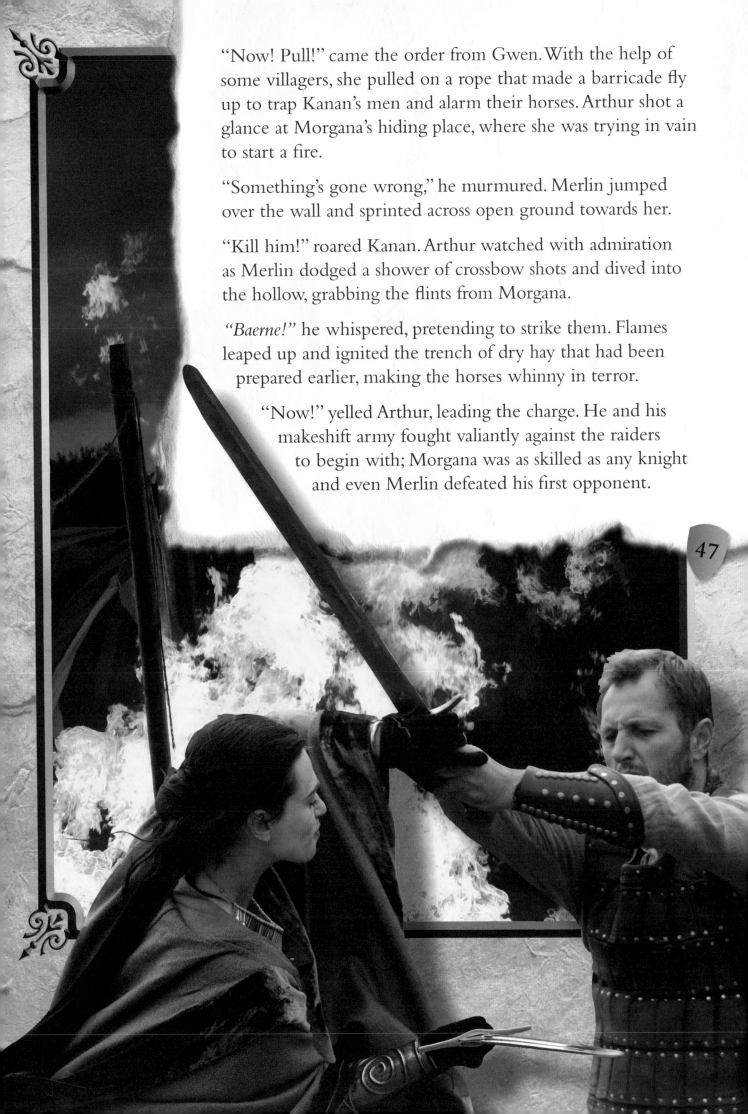

"Now! Pull!" came the order from Gwen. With the help of some villagers, she pulled on a rope that made a barricade fly up to trap Kanan's men and alarm their horses. Arthur shot a glance at Morgana's hiding place, where she was trying in vain to start a fire.

"Something's gone wrong," he murmured. Merlin jumped over the wall and sprinted across open ground towards her.

"Kill him!" roared Kanan. Arthur watched with admiration as Merlin dodged a shower of crossbow shots and dived into the hollow, grabbing the flints from Morgana.

*"Baerne!"* he whispered, pretending to strike them. Flames leaped up and ignited the trench of dry hay that had been prepared earlier, making the horses whinny in terror.

"Now!" yelled Arthur, leading the charge. He and his makeshift army fought valiantly against the raiders to begin with; Morgana was as skilled as any knight and even Merlin defeated his first opponent.

48

One of Kanan's men galloped towards Merlin, spinning his mace, but Will appeared from nowhere and knocked the rider to the ground before he could deliver the blow.

"Thanks!" exclaimed Merlin. "I didn't think you were coming!"

"Neither did I," grinned Will. The pair fought on, but it was soon clear that Kanan was gaining the upper hand. Merlin had no choice but to whisper a spell, whipping up a whirlwind so strong that any riders were snatched from their horses and hurled to the ground. By the time the wind died down, any uninjured men were fleeing . . . except Kanan.

"Pendragon!" he bellowed, lunging at the Prince with his battleaxe held high. Arthur was ready and quickly disarmed him, but the bandit grabbed a sword from one of his dead men. The two clashed blades furiously until at last the Prince landed a fatal blow and Kanan slumped to the ground.

Arthur demanded to know who had created the whirlwind, but before Merlin could answer Will yelled out a warning and pushed the prince to the floor. A crossbow shot fired by the dying Kanan hit Will squarely in the chest and he collapsed.

"You saved my life . . ." gasped Arthur.

"That's twice I've saved you," Will groaned. "I'm the one who used magic to summon the wind."

"Will, don't –" Merlin interrupted.

"You're a sorcerer?" Arthur asked shocked.

"Yeah, what're you going to do?" Will mocked. "Kill me?"

49

Arthur lowered his eyes. He knew Merlin's friend was already dying.

"Of course not," he replied softly, leaving the pair alone.

"You're a great man, Merlin," said Will, "and one day you're going to be servant to a great king."

"Thanks to you," smiled Merlin, tears trickling down his cheeks. He held Will's hand until the light faded from his eyes forever.

Merlin's loyal friend had died an honourable death. Merlin knew his secret would be safe for a little longer . . .

# A Message To Merlin

This is the coded message that Hunith sent to Merlin when Kanan's outlaws first attacked Ealdor.
Use the key to work out what it says.

a b c d e f g h i j k l

m n o p r s t u w x y z

_ _ _ _ _      _ _ _ _ _ _

_ _      _ _ _ _ _      _ _ _ _ _ _

# Gyngerbrede

Hunith could have made her guests some gyngerbrede if Kanan hadn't stolen all the grain! She would have baked hers in a stone oven, but you can use the modern one in your kitchen – preheat it to 180°C/Gas Mark 4 before you start. Don't forget to ask a grown-up to help you.

350g plain flour
175g light brown sugar
100g butter, cut into cubes
1 egg
4 tablespoons golden syrup
1 teaspoon ground ginger
1 teaspoon bicarbonate of soda

**1.** Sieve your flour into a mixing bowl.

**2.** Add the butter, ginger and bicarbonate of soda.

**3.** Use your fingertips to rub in the butter until the mixture looks like breadcrumbs and then stir in the sugar.

**4.** Mix in the syrup and egg until you have a firm dough.

**5.** Dust a clean work surface and rolling pin with flour so that you can roll out the dough to about 5 mm thick.

**6.** Use whatever shaped cutters you like to cut out your biscuits.

**7.** Put your biscuits on a greased baking tray and ask a grown-up to put them in the oven for 10-15 minutes.

# HEADING FOR HOME

Now that Ealdor is safe, it's time for Merlin and his friends to head home to Camelot. Which way should they go to get home?

# ENCHANTED EGGS

These magical eggs all look the same, but only one is the real egg that carries Nimueh's Afanc. Can you spot which one is perfect? The answer is at the back of your annual.

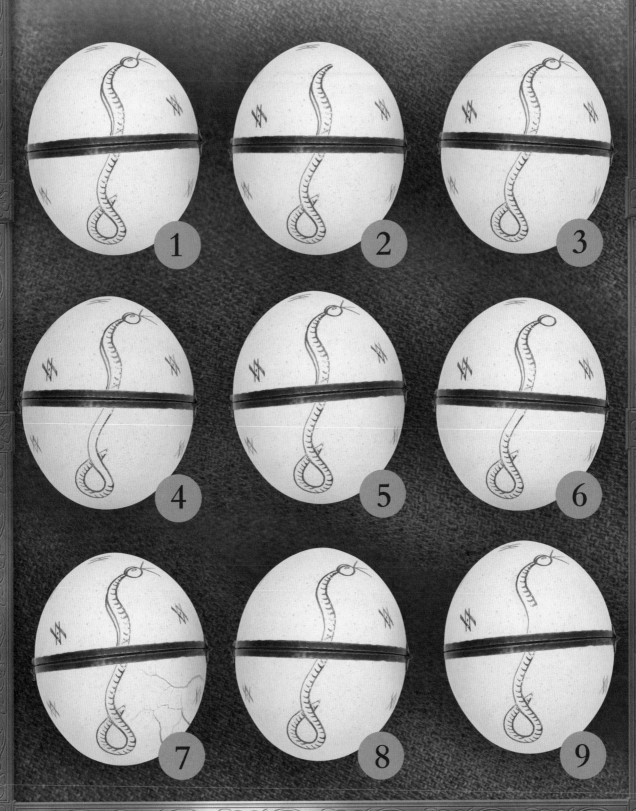

# A Physician's Notes

Gaius is a great scholar, but he is always learning new things and helping Merlin out. Take a peek at these pages from his notebook...

## Mortaeus flower poisoning

### Symptoms
convulsions
unconsciousness
respiration difficulties
high fever
weak pulse
distinctive ring~shaped purple rash

Slow and painful death follows within five days unless enchantment is present, in which case the poison will kill twice as quickly.

### Treatment
A potion made from the Mortaeus leaf, found only in the caves deep beneath the forest of Balor.
The plant grows on the roots of the Mortaeus tree and flourishes without light. Reaching it is a highly dangerous task, for a ferocious Cockatrice guards the forest and venomous spiders inhabit the caves in large numbers.

_If magic has been used to bring about the poisoning, then magic must also be used when administering the antidote._

## Notes on an Afanc

### Appearance
An Afanc is a vicious, clawed beast that is larger than a grown man. It has impenetrable skin and its teeth are sharper than the finest daggers.

### Nature
It is a creature born of clay, conjured by the most powerful sorcerers.

### Notable characteristics
Man~made weapons cannot harm an Afanc. It is made from two of the four base elements: earth and water. Only the other two, wind and fire, can destroy it. The fire must be blown towards the creature by the wind until the flames fully envelop its body and kill it.

58

# MYSTICAL CREATURES

There were all sorts of magical beasts roaming the land in Merlin's time. See if you can choose the right word from the ones below to complete each sentence. The answers are on page 61.

1. The Griffin was a creature of magic that had the head and wings of an ..........

2. The sound that the Questing Beast made was a terrifying ............

3. Arthur presented his father with the horn of a .............. as a hunting trophy.

4. Only the two elements ........... and wind could destroy an Afanc.

5. Arthur was almost attacked by giant venomous ........... in the caves beneath the forest of Balor.

6. The only sword that would kill the Black Knight was one forged in a ..........'s breath.

7. The lizard-like ............. guarded the forest of Balor.

8. It was believed that ........... fortune came to anyone who slay a unicorn.

9. The Griffin had the muscular body of a ............

10. The fearsome Questing Beast had the head of a ..............

| Cockatrice | eagle |
| bad | lion |
| unicorn | serpent |
| bark | dragon |
| spiders | fire |

59

# CREATURE CREATION

Mythical creatures of old were often grotesque hybrids of existing animals. What would your perfect magical beast look like? Would it be ferocious, like the Questing Beast, or a little friendlier, like the unicorn? Use this space to create your own mystical creature!

60

# ANSWERS

## 10 WORDSEARCH

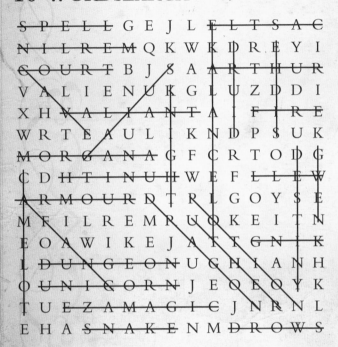

## 36 NUMBER STONES

| 153 |
| 76 | 77 |
| 39 | 37 | 40 |
| 20 | 19 | 18 | 22 |
| 9 | 11 | 8 | 10 | 12 |
| 5 | 4 | 7 | 1 | 9 | 3 |

## 37 CROSSWORD

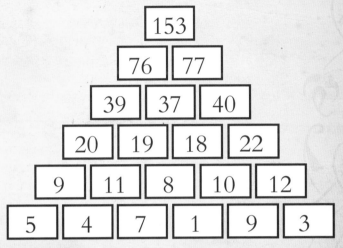

## 11 SPOT THE DIFFERENCE

## 21 THE VISITOR

Valiant came from The Western Isles.

## 24 WORDSNAKE

The leftover letters spell Gaius.

## 25 LANCELOT LETTERS

Choose from: a, at, an, on, one, all, eat, ate, lot, let, toe, oat, ant, tall, not, cell, tell, ten, ton, toll, cat, can, tan, call, ace, ale, net, cot, con, tale, clot, cone, coal, tone, note, once, loan, lean, clan, clean, lane, lance, cane, neat, lace, late, talon, alone, cello.

## 41 MEDICINE MUDDLE

1. Mint  2. Rosemary  3. Sage
4. Lavender  5. Thyme

## 50 A MESSAGE TO MERLIN

Help Ealdor is under attack

## 53 FRIEND OR FOE

1. Edwin  2. Arthur  3. Valiant  4. Anhorra
5. Morgana  6. Kanan  7. Gaius  8. Nimueh  9. Gwen

## 57 ENCHANTED EGGS

Egg 5 is the real one.

## 59 MYSTICAL CREATURES

1. eagle  2. bark  3. unicorn  4. fire  5. spiders
6. dragon  7. Cockatrice  8. bad  9. lion  10. serpent

61